MW01536927

Published by

Page One NA Inc.
Hubbard, Ohio

Copyright 2023 Michael Gammella

ISBN: 9798389118669
ISBN: 9798389118669

Cover Design: Page One NA Inc., Hubbard Ohio

Preface

Have you ever wondered why a few seem to have been born under a "Lucky Star"? The fact is we are ALL born under that star. This manuscript will show you the way. So that you may go from the many...... To the Few.

Table of Contents

Introduction

Ever since I was a little boy, I was fascinated with people. Their personalities, the way they talked, walked, their lives.

This small book are the observations I have made for over a half a century.

I have learned and observed a lot. However, the most important thing I have noted is that there are many different people in this world. Billions, but **there is only one you**. What you become is up to you.

I write this today, so that you can become yourself! Who you want to be.

So that you can lift yourself from the many and be one of the Few.

> **"Knowing yourself is the beginning of all wisdom" - Aristotle**

> *"Brevity is a great praise of eloquence"*
> *- Cicero*

This manuscript is intentionally brief. Great pains have been made to make it so.

As one sage once said... "Ask me to write a long speech and I will have it in a day. Ask for a short speech and I can write it in a week".

THE FEW

The Many and the Few.

This text is a guide to the Few. You may already be one of the Few. If so you have my heartfelt congratulations.

If you are one of the many you hold the manuscript in your hands to become one of the Few. It is your decision.

The overwhelming majority of people in this world are a part of the many.

They go about their life clueless and aimlessly. They depend on others to tell them how to live THEIR lives. They follow the crowd. They see a line and they get in it. Simply put they never master their own lives. Much less live it. They never become themselves. What they want to be! What they can be!

The Few

The Few take the time to understand life. **They Live Their Lives**. They are happy and content with who they are.

This has led many of them to be financially secure. They are wealthy not only in money but life experiences and knowledge unused by others. They are indeed rich. This small book is intentionally kept short because one of lifes secrets is that **life is short.**

This book is written so that you may become one of the Few. Not everyone will. The many will not.

The simple fact that you are reading this right now is because you have it within yourself to be happy, healthy and successful in this short journey we call life.

Remember... "At any given time, you can go from where your at, to where you want to be!

Its truly up to you! **The Decision Is Yours.**

> **"There is no worse bitterness than to reach the end of your life and realize you have not lived." - M. Scott Peck M.D.**

Take the time

Many years ago when our children were small we went on a long road trip to Naples, Florida. As I was driving furiously to get back home we passed by a huge water park, four hours from home. Our children, who had been great and very quite erupted like a volcano. Dad lets stop they all pleaded in unison. I would have none of it. I was on a mission to get back home.

They pleaded that I stop, but to no avail. I had a schedule to keep and I was keeping it. Then it hit me, we were on vacation. Why not stop. The only schedule was in my head.

The kids deserved a break after that long drive. So I turned around and went back to that water park. As fate would have it the admission price was cut in half in 15 minutes.

We waited the 15 minutes buying ice cream and then went in.

The kids had a ball for the next two hours. We ended up getting home at 9:00pm rather than the scheduled 7:00pm. I write this to say this, after two great weeks in Florida, years and years later our three children still talked about that water park and how they loved it.

Take the time, it makes a difference.

"In all of the things you want to do in life... take the time and do them."

No one in a nursing home or on their death bed ever said, "I wish I spent more time at work, in the office, at the bar, or on the couch.

Take the time to live your life. Do what you want.

Achieve and live your dreams.

The only way is to take the time and do it!

"The days drag, and the years fly by."
- Clemente Gammella

Knowing what you want

Knowing what you want out of life is of the utmost importance.

If you are not happy no one around you will be happy, and it will effect your health.

Knowing what you want is not as easy as it sounds. We are constantly bombarded daily being told what we want, by the internet, phone, TV, magazines, newspapers, strangers, family members and on and on. It is endless but how often have you taken the time to sit alone in quiet by yourself and ask yourself what do you want! Most people never do. They listen to others, the media ect. to tell them what they want. It's called marketing and peer pressure. Always remember this truth...

You cannot make other people happy if you are not happy.

You have to be happy. And you and **Only** you can make yourself happy. No one else can do it for you. The first thing you need to do is sit quietly by yourself and ask yourself what do you want in your life. Not what everyone else wants, what do you want!

Until you can answer this simple question

you will never be happy.

Remember happiness is not a destination, it is a part of the journey. The journey we call life.

| **"To yourself be true" - Socrates** |

Where do you want to go in life.

The only way to get anywhere is knowing where you want to go. The many do not see this simple truth. They spend their entire life wandering aimlessly. If you want to get somewhere you have to know where you want to go.

Until then you will never get anywhere.

When Alice in Wonderland came to the fork in the road, she asked the Cheshire Cat which road should she take, the Cheshire Cat wisely asked her (Alice) where do you want to go? When Alice (the many) informed him she did not know were she wanted to go, the cat wisely told Alice "Then any road will do."

And that's what most people do. Spend their entire lives not knowing where they want to go, and follow the trails (lives) of everyone else.

Make your own trails (Life). That's the only way to get where you want to go.

> **"Follow your heart and intuition, they somehow already know what you truly want to become. Everything else is secondary" - Steve Jobs Co-Creator Apple Computer**

Health

Your Greatest asset is your health. If you were born healthy, consider yourself very fortunate.

Many are not so fortunate. Yet they can and do still live good lives.

Keeping yourself healthy is of extreme importance. Remember you cannot be physically healthy if you are not mentally healthy.

The mind has a lot to do with your physical health.

Get plenty of sleep, meditate, give yourself alone time. Do not smoke. Do not drink to excess. Do not over eat. Drink at least 32 oz of water per day. See a doctor twice a year for a check up. Even if nothings wrong. Remember even the worst disease can be cured if its caught quickly enough.

Exercise and stay active all thru your life. Be happy and content with your life. To quote Cicero...

"A Life of peace and purity, and refinement leads to an untroubled and calm old age" - Cicero 83BC

Health is your greatest wealth. And health is a by product of happiness.

Your Friends

Many years ago on Tuesday nights after work my friends and I would meet at a local tavern to have drinks and food. We were all friends and colleagues. However, I noticed something early on. We would all be laughing and joking. But as soon as someone got up to go to the restroom, they became the topic of ridicule and scorn.

As soon as they came back, they were great again. This happened to every single person. Including me.

Friends are not always your friends. They are to your face, but behind your back look out. If you move ahead of them in anyway in jobs, money, spouse, house ect, ect, they will become resentful of you. Hence the old saying "Misery Loves Company".

I know a lot of people, who think they have many friends. What they have are a lot of acquaintances and colleagues. But few, very few friends.

The so called friends will hold you back on your journey to spiritual growth and success. Understand who you hang with today, your "friends" of today, will become your memories of tomorrow.

> **"He who travel fastest, travels alone."**
> **- Rudyard Kipling**

I have found this proverb to be very true. Do not let your friends hold you back. Proceed with your life.

Remember when you follow the crowd, you go where the crowds going. Nowhere!

Live where you want to live.

You have choices in life.

One of the biggest and least understood is where do you want to live.

Some people like the coasts, some the mountains, some like it hot, some like it cold and some moderate. You should strive to live where you want to live. It may be something so simple as a change of neighborhood or as exotic as an island in the Pacific. Choose where you want to live. Yes it may cost you more money to live there. But why spend your money living in a place you hate? Today you can work remotely from almost anywhere with no commute.

It's Important to be happy.

Live where you want! It's your life.

In the long run you will spend less money because you will be happy, content, healthier and most likely more productive. Live your life. Many people "go out" just to escape their homes. Home is home. It is where you should want to be. Live where you want to! It's important to your spiritual and mental health. Pick a place and become a part of that community.

> "...Far and away the most important thing in life is living it...".
> — Frank R. Barry

Hate

Nothing destroys <u>YOU</u> quicker than hate. When you hate it comes back to you multiplied. When others hate you the same thing happens to them.

Ask yourself, have you ever known a hateful person that was happy? Most even hate themselves and this is totally self destructive. Let your hate go!

Don't forget, but release that hate inside of you. President Richard Nixon summed it up best in his farewell address to his White House Staff...

"Always do your best. Never be petty. Others may hate you but they don't win until you hate them back, because then you destroy yourself." - R.N. President Richard Nixon.

A wise man. I could not say it any better. Hate destroys the hater.

Again, nothing destroys YOU quicker than hate!

Your Spouse

One of the most, if not the most important decisions you will make is who you will marry and spend the rest of your life with. Many will snicker at this previous sentence and that is exactly the problem. People take the bonds of marriage far to lightly.

Most don't look for a mate, they look for a status symbol.

Marry someone you truly like and enjoy being with. Someone who shares your goals and desires.

If you decide to marry, marry when you want to marry. In every marriage there are ups and downs. Just like life. It is not perfect. However marrying the right person for you will give you the most happiness and joy throughout your life. Remember the grass is not always greener elsewhere. Stay married, stay committed, to both your spouse and your children. This will pay you far greater dividends than money. Besides if you are happy, you need far less money.

If you cannot make this commitment, do not get married. Marriage is not for everyone. A long engagement is best.

If you decide to marry try to wait before having children. Divorce between two adults is bad enough. However, when children are involved its the end of their world. Just be very mindful of who you marry and why. And if your just marrying for money or looks, you have chosen the wrong reasons.

Marry well and your life will go well.

Remember... Happy Spouse, Happy House.

Children

Children are a wonderful thing to have. Yet they are not for everyone. This includes many who have them. The many only think of themselves, not their offspring. They prepare their children as they prepare themselves... Unprepared. If you want children you must be ready to put in the love and time for them. To educate them, teach them and put their needs before your own. As with your spouse you must be totally dedicated. The Few are.

And remember, let children be children. They will have plenty of time to be adults later on in life. Many adults problems stem from not being able to be a child.

And most importantly...

Children need to know they are loved and valued! Listen to your children. Spend time with them and do things with them. Take them places with you. And learn from them as they will learn from you. Your actions will speak far louder than your words. Late in life you will be glad you spent time with them, and so will they!

Stress

Stress is a killer! Everyone has some stress in their lives. However, Excessive stress can and will open you up to a lot of diseases and heartache.

Avoid stress as much as you can. If someone or something is causing you excessive stress, GET IT OUT OF YOUR LIFE! <u>It maybe hard to do, but its killing you and what is worse than that</u>? Sometimes its easy. I once read a single mom always woke up tired, always late, and had to drive to work like she was on a motor speedway. It was **EXTREMELY STRESSFUL** and the worst part of her day. Not to speak of how unsafe it was. Her solution? As she herself said in this article.... "I started waking up 45 minutes earlier. I was still tired however I was no longer in a hurry or stressed out in my driving."

A simple solution and it worked.

Think about what in your life makes you stressful and how you can eliminate it. Only you can do it. **And you can!**

Your job (How you earn income)

How you earn your income is important. The majority will get a job. Some will start their own business, some will live off trust funds or the government.

Which ever way you choose to earn your income is up to you. However, it is important to enjoy what you do. I started on an assembly line.

I hated it. Yet I kept working to find a job I liked. You can to.

When you find a job you like, it may pay less money, however if you truly enjoy it you will find a way to make more money. There or elsewhere. **In doing what you want to do.**

When you have a job you enjoy, you will not need as much money to be happy.

Always remember you are a free agent in life. Do what works for you! Go to a sporting event or a concert. People are paying big money to be there. Yet the ushers, security and so on are being paid to be there.

And you know what? They are the least happy. Because in their minds they are working. And they are, yet they are still listening to the music, watching the game, being where the action is. My point is they should be enjoying their job. But most are not.

Now let them by a high priced ticket and they love being there. Same place, same situation, its the way you think and look at the world. It's all a mindset. Strive to make your living in something you enjoy doing. A wise person once said...

If you do what you enjoy, you will never work again. A job that pays the most might not be the best for you.

> **"People spend more time making a living than creating a life" - Dolly Parton**

How much money do you really need?

The answer to this question varies widely with your age, family, where you live and how you want to live. For example, if you want your own private jet you need far more than the person willing to fly commercial. The point is, try to accumulate the amount of money you and your family needs to live a comfortable life. Comfortable and rich are two very different things. The bible is often misquoted by people who state "Money is the root of all evil." What the bible states is "The **Love** of money is the root of all evil" That's a huge difference. Money is not the root of all evil! Everyone needs it to survive. The love of money is greed plain and simple. And greed in any form is bad. The root of all evil!

Greedy people are not happy people. They may pretend to be with their obnoxious wealth however they are flawed. The person who can live with and be happy with the least is truly the wealthy person. Find out what you need and go out and get it. There is one sure way to never attain what you need. And that is to follow the many and never try. As quoted in the bible.. "Ask and you shall receive" Know what you want in life. Set goals and you will achieve it.

> **To quote the Rolling Stones....**
> **"You can't always get what you want, but if you try sometimes you'll find you get what you need"**

The lesson is to set goals and try. You will succeed as long as you are true to yourself.

> **"We make a living by what we get, but we make a life by what we give".**
> **- Winston Churchill**

Pay yourself first!

Save and Invest 10% of your money every year. The only way to obtain financial stability is to save and invest 10% of your yearly income. You do this by one simple method... PAY YOURSELF FIRST! Before you pay anyone or anything pay yourself first! Sound easy? It's not. Everyone wants your hard earned money, Everyone! The landlord, the bank, the credit cards, stores, bars & restaurants, insurance companies, taxes, family, friends and the list goes on. But think about this for 30 seconds. Should you not pay the most important person first? YOU! The many give their money to everyone and everything else but themselves. And here's the rub. They have the money. Obviously they are paying everyone else with it. But not themselves. They keep themselves in a trap of negative prosperity. Albert Einstein Stated..

> **"Interest, those who do not understand it pay it. Those who do understand it profit from it." - Albert Einstein**

By paying yourself first you will profit from it. Currently in America the best place you can put your long term savings in a Standard & Poors index fund. (The overall stock market) Keep it there!

Do not worry about the ups and downs. Keep investing in it and you will prosper at retirement time.

> **No one is more important than you! Pay Yourself First!**

Manners & Politeness

Manners and Politeness go a long way in our society. Some call it respect. Whatever you call it, use it!

Always treat people the way you want to be treated. This is a simple thing to do. But the many never do it. The Few do.

And its one huge reason they are more successful and happy. **Respect Yourself first** and foremost and everyone around you. As the old saying goes "What goes around, comes around." Nothing is more true.

"Manners are a sensitive awareness of the feelings of others. If you have that awareness you have good manners, no matter what fork you use" - Emily Post

Random Acts of Kindness

Perform random acts of kindness. When you see someone in need help them if you can safely!

This does not apply to beggars. Thats the job they've chosen. You would be shocked at how much a good beggar makes a week. Especially in the right spot. I always pass on beggar's. I tip very well to working people.

Do simple little things that go a long way in making other peoples day a little easier. For instance if your at the checkout counter at the store with a lot of items and the person behind you has one or two items, let them go ahead of you. You will be surprised at how people appreciate this small gesture. Recently after a bad snowstorm I noticed the guy up the street from me struggling to shovel his snow. I took my snowblower and finished his driveway for him. Go to a nursing home to visit someone you know. It goes a long way.

Hold a door open for someone. If you practice random acts of kindness, in a short time you will notice your life has gotten a little better to.

"The only gift that you can keep is one you give." Maude Park

---

Technology

Technology is great, without it we would be stagnant. It is also advancing more rapidly than you think.

The general public is 20 to 30 years behind todays technological advances. Keep the fax machine and color television in mind.

They both took decades before reaching the general public. Technology is there for you to use.

Sadly in most cases, technology uses the very people it was meant to help. Many have become addicted to their phones and computers. Their world is the world of facebook and the internet. Not the real world.

What keeps us ahead of technology is that we are human beings, The creators of technology. However the many are becoming less and less human. Just look at how the many treat each other. And most importantly how many treat themselves. If you treated them like they treat themselves they would hate you.

This is where technology and social media take over. They are no longer individuals. They have become part of the net. The internet. And are all thinking in lockstep (like the old assembly lines). The problem is that technology is doing their thinking for them. Once artificial intelligence realizes this they (or it) may become our masters. We will do your thinking for you. After all, we work for you. We are only machines. You humans are the true masters. But for how long? This is why it is critical to be a true person. Your own person. Use technology, however make certain that it is not using you or spying on you.

Use technology, do not allow it to use you!

What is true wealth?

Having only money and power is not true wealth. Many posses money and power and they are miserable at there core. Health is wealth, happiness is wealth, being one is great wealth. Helping others and caring about others and this world we all live in is enlightenment! A great source of wealth. Money will not buy you happiness, it will buy you temporary pleasures. Just think of something you really wanted and got. Does it still make you happy today, or has another need or greed taken its place. True wealth stays with you. You are appreciative and grateful for it. Yes money is important. Greed and excess is not.

To be truly wealthy you have to be happy. You have to be content. How can you be miserable and consider yourself rich? Rich in what? Consumer luxury items. The most expensive automobile and the least expensive automobile will get you to the same place.

The difference is that if you are unhappy and insecure you need a luxury automobile. This is how they (and most) define themselves and others by what they drive or wear. Those who need the least will be happiest.

Opulence and excessive luxury are only a way to show off. To show others what they have, and most importantly to show you what you don't have. Many (most) were born into this luxury. They did nothing to achieve it. Yet they feel (or know) that they are better than everyone else.

They define themselves in their monetary status to others. A millionaire always wishes they were a billionaire. There are people whose fiscal statements say who they are. True wealth is not the size of your bank account. It is a well lived and deserved life of happiness and bringing happiness to others. It is good health, the correct mental attitude and content with your life in your heart and soul.

Insecure people need to show off. The many fall for it, the Few do not.

> **"Having is not always as pleasurable as wanting. It is not logical, yet I have often found it to be true."**
> **- Mr. Spock, Star Trek**

Don't Worry

If you can't control something DO NOT WORRY ABOUT IT. If you can control it, fix it to what you want. Worry is one of the most destructive things people do to themselves. (Hate is still by far #1) they worry so much about what people say about them or how others view them, that they can never be happy. They worry about trivial or non essential things like will their sports team win or not.

Never worry. Especially if its a medical condition because worry will always make it worse. Doctors will tell you, a positive mental attitude goes a long way in determining your health. The body and mind are linked.

What the mind tells the body over time, the body will eventually believe.

Remember this truism....

PEOPLE SPEND THEIR LIVES, WORRYING ABOUT THINGS THAT NEVER HAPPEN.

If you cannot control it, don't worry about it.

"I do not have the luxury to worry. It stops me from solving problems."
                    - WM Cafaro Sr., Magnate

No one can hurt you emotionally but you!

We all have trials and tribulations in this journey we call life. Some people enjoy hurting others feelings. There is nothing worse than being jilted by one you love. It hurts a lot. Even family and so called friends will hurt you emotionally. Do not give them this power over you! Move on with your life without those who hurt you. Remember the only time they can hurt you is when you allow it. This takes a lot of meditation, soul searching, prayer and self discipline but you can get to that level in life where your emotions will no longer hurt you. It is called growth and strength. **It is within you, it is within all of us!** As with most other things, most people never take the time to learn these life truths.

Be the master of your own fate. Follow yourself, never the many.

Sleep

Everyones sleeping pattern is different. Some people need more sleep, some less. Some "experts" will tell you to get 8 hours of sleep per night. No more no less. You are far better of with more sleep than 8 hours. **I have never woke up in the morning wishing I went to bed later.** Sleep is the time that your body rests, but most importantly the time your mind rests and your subconscious. If you have a problem or question as to what action to take, **Sleep On It**. This is nothing new. For centuries people with decisions to make have stated "Let me sleep on it". Before going to sleep while laying in bed ask the question you have to yourself in your mind or out loud. Ask for help solving it. Then go to sleep. Sleep on it. Most of the time the answer will come to you as you lie there, when you dream or when you first awake in the morning.

The morning time is extremely critical for answers, new ideas and clairvoyance. Just before you are fully awake lie there and think. You will be amazed at what will come to you. As said in the bible "Ask and you shall receive." You will receive an answer. It may take 2 or 3 mornings or evenings but an answer will come. And it will be the correct and proper answer.This is what wise people do. **They listen for answers.**

The many do not. First thing in the morning they look at their phones and emails. They do not listen or think at this critical time of the day. By listening to those morning thoughts before you are out of bed will improve your day and efficiency. You will get more accomplished. **Just listen to your inner thoughts**. Also, early in the morning after you get out of bed, make a simple list of what you want to do or accomplish on that day. When you accomplish an item, cross it off and go on to the next item. This is very important since you are telling your subconscious you are listening to it and resolving issues.

You will find by making out this simple list every morning in about 5 minutes you will get more done. This is a very simple yet effective way of goal setting and it works. Remember, if you do not know where you are going, you will never get to where you want to go! **It's all up to you**. Nobody makes the list but you!

<u>Remember, It's your life and it's your responsibility to live it</u>. Sleep, rest and meditation are essential to putting your mind into a higher plain of thought. The many never do.

That's why they go no further than one another. The Few like you move ahead and are far healthier and happier. The reason I said "Like You" in the preceeding sentence is the fact that you have read this book to this point. Only a few will. The answers are not in video games, phones, technology, gossip and so on. They are in this book that you are reading.

Congratulations on reading this far. Because the secrets are about to be revealed to you in the next chapters. Only you and the Few will garner this knowledge. It's so simple yet so effective. You cannot teach genius in school. But you will learn to think like one here. It is quite appropriate that these last few sentences have been placed in a chapter called sleep.

The many sleepwalk thru life. The Few live rich and happy lives. It's all in your mindset. The next few chapters will open doors for you that the many will never believe exist.

Be Prepared.

Prepare yourself! Remember that old adage…" An ounce of prevention , is worth a pound of cure." Being prepared and thinking ahead makes your life FAR smoother. However the many do not prepare. I learned this lesson when I was 16 years old working the counter at McDonalds. Back then McDonalds was just starting to open restaurants nation wide. When they came to your neighborhood or town it was a big deal. People flocked there. On Friday nights (Payday) from 5 until 7 P.M. there were LONG LINES completely out the doors. People would wait 15 or 20 minutes to get to the counter to order dinner. And when they FINALLY did here's how it would go…….. I would cheerfully say "Good evening Sir (or Ma'am) may I take your order please." And they would respond…." Yes… Now let me see." They would then stare at the huge menu board behind the counter **that was in front of them the entire time in line**, study it, and then SLOWLY proceed to give their order. Usually changing it a few times. Even then not quite certain what they wanted.

THE FEW, and I mean VERY few knew exactly what they wanted. Some even had it written down. The FEW were prepared, the many were not. So goes their lives in this small example.

Be Grateful

Above all, be grateful for what you have. If you want more, and follow the practices in this book you will get more. However, **At All Times** be grateful for what you have. Being grateful alone will set you above the many. Take the time everyday in the morning before you get out of bed, and when you lie down to go to bed to say thank you for all you have. Just say it to the voice, that intuition in your mind that spans all universal knowledge and power. Say it a few times a day (3 to 4). Being grateful is a way of saying thank you. A universal way. Ungratefulness causes many problems. In yourself, your family, employer and government. Next to hate, worry, and greed nothing causes more harm to yourself, loved ones and the entire world than individuals not appreciative for what they currently have. Again you may and should want more. But you must be grateful to what you already have. That is the only way to achieve more. Just be grateful. It's easy. The Few are grateful. The many only look at what's wrong with their lives. Never what is right in their life. And the cause of what's wrong is usually themselves.

Wishing, Asking For & Visualization

Wishes do come true. Ask any successful and happy person.

You cannot "just wish" you must believe in your wishes". Napoleon Hill wrote "whatever you can conceive and believe you can achieve". No computer or technology is more intelligent than the human mind. **IF USED PROPERLY.** The problem is the many barely scratch the surface of what they are capable of. They have the power within them. They never use it. Sadly they do not even try. What is fascinating is that the Few who do, come from the many. Why do we take such bold steps forward while they take steps back or stay stagnant? What triggers the quest for knowledge. The many for the most part are educated, well trained, fine employees and good people yet they remain in the many. The problem is they do not take the time to think, meditate and listen to their very own receiver known as the brain. Children are taught at a very young age that wishes do not come true, you cannot get what you ask for and you cannot just visualize you must work.

Yes, you must work, but work without a

purpose or a plan is running the many into a circle. A brief example is in order here. When elephants are babys, a chain is applied to their legs and staked into the ground. The baby elephant soon learns that no matter how many times it tugs on the chain it cannot go any further. For months and months this lesson is applied until it comes to the point where the elephant feels the tug of the chain they just stop automatically knowing they can go no further. Even the largest elephants do this because this is what they are **TAUGHT** thru their experience. Little do they know that once adults they could easily pull the stake from the ground. They just go as far as that tug. Because that's what they were taught by example as youngsters.

Do not allow yourself to be "staked down" by old thoughts.

To quote the great inventor Thomas Edison...

"If we did all of the things we are capable of doing, we would literally astound ourselves." - Thomas Edison

---

We must unite as a planet

<u>We are one planet, and yes one people</u>. We need to come together as one planet and people. Nationalism leads to war, prejudice and mistrust.

A constant barrage thru history of us against them. **WE ARE ALL THE US AND THE THEM.** Both the many and the Few.

The sooner we learn this the better off we will all be.

Perhaps in a few thousand years we will be a united planet. It will be essential to our survival and acceptance as a species.

> **"Our basic common link is that we all inhabit the same planet. We all breathe the same air. We all cherish our children's future. And we are all mortal"**
> **- John F. Kennedy Past U.S. President**

Time

There is nothing more important to your life than time. How you use it and deal with it will shape your success and happiness. A very long time ago I penned this poem...

"I'm here, I'm there, I'm everywhere. I pass without motion, I pass without sound. You never see or hear me yet I'm always around and depending how you use me, I'm either your enemy or best friend.

But one thing is certain. In this life I'm all you have. Do you Know who I am?....Time."

The many never pay attention or respect time. The Few do. We understand that time is really all we have. Without time, what is there?

Use your time here wisely. The fact that you even acknowledge times presence, places you with the Few. Time is youth, it is then middle age, then if we are fortunate it becomes old age.

If you grow in life you will have a peaceful and contented old age. If you do not grow in life spiritually and to become a better person your old age will be full of regret and bitterness.

> "Your time here is limited. So don't waste it living someone else's life."
> - Steve Jobs, Co-Creator Apple Computer

> "It's already tomorrow today."
> - Anthony D'Amico

> **" You must not only go through life, you must grow thru life."**
>   **- Eric Butterworth**

Their is much to rob you of your time. Television, computers, cell phones, sporting events along with video games, facebook, reality TV, instagram, snap chat and on and on. And things that have not even been invented yet.

All designed to be addictive and to steal your time and stop you from thinking. Demanding your attention and eventually selling you and your data! Making money off you. What you eat, buy, like, talk to, associate with. All collected on your time. You essentially are working for them. For free. You can use your time far better than this. A wise man once told me "The days drag, yet the years fly by." And the older you get, the quicker time flies. Everything you learn and do over time is important. Even failure. **If you have not failed, you have not tried. And not even trying is the greatest failure of all.**

Do this exercises while laying in your bed. Morning or night.

Think to yourself, if you were confined to this bed, if this was your last few minutes of life, what would you wish you would have done.

The answer may surprise you.

One day you will be in that position and there will be nothing you can do about it. However, today you can! Do that thing you really want to do. It's called "A leap of faith". It is extremely important to your growth and happiness as a human being. Act while you still have the time and health to act!

Thought without action is useless. Seize the time while you can.

If you think old, you will act old, you will be old. Think young and determined. Never loose that zest for life at anytime. Sadly the many loose this zest very young and early in life. They simply don't believe they can live the life they want. Time to them is their enemy. Always wanting time to pass, as they do nothing with it. It has been said there are three types of people in this world....

People who make things happen.

Those who watch things happen.

And then the many, who wonder what happened.

Make the very most of your time. Employers, the media, government, your friends and relatives all steal your time. True you have to give them some of it... But not all of it.

Take time for you. To sit quietly undisturbed in a quiet spot. And let your mind wander. Listen to what is being said to you thru a sort of universal telepathy in your mind. I call it "The Voice".

If you sit quietly, alone for 20 minutes in the morning or afternoon and 20 minutes at night you will notice a marked difference in your thought pattern and the way you perceive things. You will be on the road of the Few. As you take more time alone, you will find during longer periods that you will become more relaxed and intune with your world. Problems will be solved or you may realize there really is not a problem at all. You may see in some cases you are the problem. Think about how you can become the solution and not the problem. And remember, **If you can afford to buy your way out of a problem, you don't have a problem.** No one is perfect, everyone errors. It's taking ownership of a problem that is the beginning in solving the problem.

When you do this, you will find your life far less stressed and aggravated.

Again the power of the Few is within you! It is up to you which path you take. Use your time wisely. It is your most precious asset.

> **To quote Cicero..**
> **"Anyone can make a mistake, but only an idiot persists in their error.**

Goals Set Them! Freedom Achieve It!

Always know what you want. If you do not know what you want go within yourself thru quiet time, prayer and meditation.

Think back to when you were a young child. What did you want your life to be like?

The only way to get what you want out of your life is to set goals. See where you want to go and make a plan to get there. It does not have to be a detailed plan. Just an idea of your plan. Know where you want to go. You very well will be swimming against the many. That negative current that wants to take you down with them and keep you down! You must be brave enough and strong enough to follow your own wishes. In some societies, religion and government they want you to be what they want you to be. If you are in this situation and many of you are you must hide your intentions or pay a heavy price. Make your move toward your freedom when you can.

Your instincts will tell you when that time is. And most importantly do not tell anyone! Many have been ruined by there so called friends or relatives. Tell no one and act alone. Act as if you cannot fail.

You must be both bold and swift. By the time they realize what you have done you will be gone. Gone to your new life.

Remember the overwhelming majority of the time, **it is not the plan that fails, but the failure to plan**. Your plan is fluid. It can and will change to circumstances. The key is that your plan still moves you to your goal. Your freedom may come as unexpected opportunity. This is Fate! Seize It!

> **"Each of us is the architect of our own fate." - Caecus**

You will be stagnant if you do not know where you are going. It's akin to taking a road trip with no destination or purpose in mind. Remember if you do not know where your going. You will never get there! Have a plan.

> **To quote the composer Curtiss Mayfield..**
> **"Your only scheme is your dream, go out and do it. Move on up."**

> **And a quote from Cicero again....**
> **What is freedom? The power to live as one wishes!**

Plan Ahead! Even Loosely!

Always Ask - Always Try

If you don't ask, you will never get.

This goes for the spiritual world and this world. You will be surprised how much more you can get by just asking. Even that person you would like to go out with. Just ask. One thing is for certain, if you do not ask it will never happen.

This goes for everything. Including prices. Always ask for their best price or better yet give them your best price. At the very worst, your going to just pay the original price anyway.

I cannot emphasize asking enough.

From houses, cars, jewelry ect. Just ask. Give them your best price. Some time ago, I sold a exotic sports car I owned. When I first owned it, it was a pleasure. After awhile it became a pain. You could not just park it anywhere even insured. It would be very difficult to replace. So I put it up for sale. One guy called to come over to look at it. He came over on time. Looked the car over, never test drove it and told me joke after joke.

He asked me for a glass of water and went and sat down on my patio. This guy is a nut I thought. I got him his water, a few more jokes and just when I was ready to ask him to leave he says will you take $$$$$$ for the car. It was less than I wanted, but I also wanted it gone. He said we could go to the bank right now and he would give me a bank check. Stunned I agreed. The point is he asked and he got the car for **his price**. Even though my ad said firm!

I often wonder if the jokes were a part of his negotiating tactics or just him. I later learned it was just him. He asked and got what he wanted and I got what I wanted.

So ask. It doesn't hurt. And if someone is offended fine. You can still pay their price if you choose to. This even work's in job promotions. Even if not quite qualified... Ask, try.

Always remember, Babe Ruth was one of the greatest home run hitters in baseball. But he struck out a lot to. No one remembers his many strikeouts. They do remember his home runs. Not one would have been possible if he did not swing the bat.

In your life you will regret what you did not do far more than what you did do.

ALWAYS TRY AND ALWAYS ASK. Even if it's for just a better table in a restaurant.

Think Long Term

Do not be shortsighted with your life. With todays medicine you may well live to be 100. More and more people are. A lot has to do with how you take care of yourself. The ancient Greeks said "All things in moderation" much has to do with how you think and relate to the world.

Many are "in Shape" physically, but not mentally. You should be both. In shape physically does not mean a "health nut". Walk, swim, lift weights moderately or other such devices. Do at least 45 minutes to an hour a day of doing something active. Especially walking, great thoughts will come to you. Even yard work and some housework counts. The point is to stay active.

I once had the pleasure of talking to the oldest employee in the city. She was 104 years old and still working. In great shape both mentally and physically. I asked her secret to good longevity and she said this... "Keep Moving! Most people when they retire just go sit and watch TV on the couch and a year later of doing that they cannot get off that couch." Many of the successful and happy seniors have told me the same thing. They all had one other trait in common, they were all young at heart.

You should plan and think to be in this category. Do not let a date just tell you how old you are.

Let your body, mind and spirit. You need to think **Long Term**. In both finances and health. Allow me to relay a true story for you concerning your finances. Many years ago I would watch the stock market, study the stock market and then buy selected stocks. I did OK, for instance buy at $10.00 per share, sell at $20.00 per share. And on and on. My wife purchased the very same stocks I did. The difference was she held them.

One day many years later as I was cleaning out our file cabinet, I noticed the stocks I doubled my money on were worth a lot more than that today. Her buy good quality and hold strategy **Easily** bested my buy and sell strategy.

It then came to me that she was indeed an investor. I was a trader making brokerage houses rich, I was almost a gambler. I will end this with a simple sentence of investment advice that took me 50 years to learn...

Buy the S&P 500 index fund, contribute to it monthly **especially** during down periods, and forget about it!

When you retire, you will be glad you did. This gives you great diversity in your holdings. **Again Think Long Term.** In your health and in your wealth and with your spouse. Think Long Term!

The Few do! That's how we get ahead and stay ahead.

> **"I skate to where the puck is going. Not to where it has been." - Wayne Gretzky, Hockey Great**

Listen

You have two ears and one mouth for a reason. **Listen not just with your ears but with your intuition.** This is your "Third Ear" the big ear. Which allows you to hear things and feel things. Learn to listen to this ear as well. By listening you are in tune with what is going on around you.

The many love to talk (babble actually). They never really say anything meaningful or constructive but in their parochial minds, they are always right. They babble, but they never listen.

If they did, their lives would be far more gratifying. Listen to people when they speak. Make note of the facial expressions and body language. When something is important or critical repeat it back to that person exactly what they just told you for conformation. This does two things. It shows the other person you heard and understand them. And it tells you exactly what you heard so you are certain of no misunderstandings.

During this time, listen with your third ear. Your intuition. What is it telling you. Is it saying this person is truthful?

Make no rash decisions just listen and learn. <u>If you let people just talk and not interrupt them you will be surprised at what they will tell you</u>. Just hold eye contact and nod occlusionally. **And let them talk**. You listen, You learn nothing when you speak. You learn everything when you listen. Both from that person speaking, and your intuition.

Follow your intuition. Some call this a "gut feel" or a "hunch" this is your third ear picking things up. **Do Not Take It Lightly**. More often than not, it is going to be correct. By taking this course of action. (yes listening is an action) you will be far ahead of the many. Listen not only to what is said, but what is not said.

This will tell you a lot. Fine tune your listening skills. You will be grateful you did. Plus you will find yourself talking less and learning more from others.

> **"Watch what people do, not just what they say. Hence the old saying, Actions speak louder than words."**

Think
Take the time to think.

When you think things thru, it will make your course of action far easier, smoother and successful. Sit quietly alone and do this. It can be in your parked car, empty office, your home. Anywhere where you can be safe and alone. Thoughts and idea's will come to you. Do not discount them.

They may literally be more valuable than gold. **REMEMBER <u>EVERYTHING</u> AROUND YOU CAME FROM A THOUGHT OR AN IDEA**!

> **"There comes a point where the mind takes a higher plain of knowledge, but can never prove how it got there. ALL great discoveries have involved such a leap."- Albert Einstein**

Think, it will all come to you.

> **Thinking is the talking of the soul with itself" - Plato**

Let Things Go

Learn to let go! When something bad happens, it already happened. Do not relive it time and time again. You are only hurting yourself. The art of letting go will free you from despair, heartbreak, agonizing, hate and so on. By letting go, you become the bigger person and the **liberated** person.

It will change your life for the better. So let go what hurts you. **Remember forgive but never forget.** But let it go and not be a daily nuisance and pain to you.

When you let go, you free yourself.

Be Yourself

No one in this world is like you. We are all unique and born are own person.

Sadly, the governments and businesses of the world do not want unique free thinking people. They want what I refer to as "Many". The many follow others. Whatever the latest trend, fashion, look, thought, politics, religion or whatever the many are doing, They Do! They do not think, they just do it to fit in. To be cool, "liked" and have what passes as friends.

The many are all things to all people. Whatever it takes. They have sold their substance their uniqueness to the "society" to which they belong. Take a look at the world around you. This country is better than that country, this religion is better, this race is better and so on and so forth. The fact is none of it is better. You are better because you are you. It is very hard being yourself while everyone else around you is trying to be someone else.

What will make you a success, what will give you the greatest piece of mind, what will make you the happiest is being yourself. Be the person you are.

If you cannot please yourself, if you are not yourself, nothing can or will ever please you.

As Socrates said, "To yourself be true.

The many are not true to themselves. They are the pawns of others. And they blame others for their unhappiness and failure.

Be a True Person! Be who you are! If you do not know who you are, do not feel bad. The many have no idea who they are. The huge difference is that you want to find yourself. The fact you are reading these lines proves that! And you can find yourself thru thought, quiet time, meditation and prayer. This is not mystic, it is fact! It is not hard, it is quite easy and natural.

We, in the Few, all have our unique and different ways of doing this. However, it is available to anyone who wants to find themselves. They're true self, the only self that will bring happiness and contentment to your life. It is covered in the upcoming chapters of Alone, Intuition, Infinite Intelligence and God.

You have come this far in these pages. Turning the page, you will learn the way of the Few.

But first the wise words of Steve Jobs, co/creator of Apple...

> **"Here is to the crazy ones, the misfits. The round pegs in the square hole. They move the human race forward. Because the crazy ones, the ones who believe they can change the world for the better do!"**
> **- Steve Jobs**

Alone

> **"All of humanity's problems stem from man's inability to sit quietly in a room alone" - Blaise Pascal**

Genius comes to you when you are sitting quietly alone. It can also come when you are walking, swimming, cycling or jogging. The point is it comes when you are alone and with your own thoughts. Many call this meditation or prayer. What ever you chose to call it... It works! Prayer is when you talk to God, meditation (quiet time) is when you listen to God and the universal Infinite Intelligence. Napoleon Hill was commissioned by the great steel magnate Andrew Carnegie perhaps the richest man of his time, to write down his secret formula of success.

That book is titled "Think and Grow Rich." In it, he reveals Carnegie's greatest secret. That is **Infinite Intelligence**. It is all around us. Anyone can tap into it. Yet only the Few do.

I call it the voice.

Here is how it works. Sit quietly and alone, think about your problem, question or dilemma. Then in your mind ask for your answer. Then continue to sit in silence as though you are meditating. No fancy breathing, no certain position, no chants. Just sit quietly for your answer. 20 minutes should do it. If you get no answer try later on, or in the evening as you lay in bed or the morning before you get out of bed. Your answer will come.

Some get a "tingle" when it does. You may or may not. Remember everyone is different. It may just pop into your head, or be in something you read or see.

But the answer will come. Infinite Intelligence is what plugs us into the universe. A new dimension and a much higher train of thought. More on this later. But the only way to reach it is through being alone and quiet with yourself. To yourself be true. It is very important, critical importance to take 7 minutes before you start your day. You can take this 7 minutes while having coffee at home or before you get out of bed. You can even take it in your car before or after driving. 7 simple minutes. Just clear your mind and let your thoughts run wild. No matter how unimportant these thoughts may seem, **Let Them Run!**

You will find yourself more relaxed and in-tuned. Do the same thing in the evening or late afternoon. Take 20 simple minutes or more of quiet time to yourself. You may even do it in the bathtub or shower. The key is alone and silent. No radio, TV, computer, cell phone, kids, spouse or friends. Just You Alone! **Your Time To Yourself.**

The many never give themselves this simple and productive luxury. It's always someone else's business their concerned with. Be concerned with your own. Your thoughts make you what you are. What you will become. Never let negative thinking destroy you. Rise above it and move away from it.

Quiet time, your time is what separates the Few from the many. It is there for everyone, yet only the Few will take the time to use it.

> **Quiet & Alone is when the greatest genius comes." - Nikola Tesla**

> **"You only grow when you are alone"**
> **- Paul Newman**

News

What passes for news today is mainly nonsense. Never good. Always bad. As they say in the news business... "If it bleeds, it leads."

They dredge up the very worst in humanity. And for only a few seconds or minutes. Then its on to the next catastrophe. Then its what movie or new game is not making any money or is making big money.

Who's running around with who, wars (the most useless curse on mankind). Then theres the commercials in the news. These ads are designed to appear where the hosts dined last night, what they drive, what to wear, etc, etc, etc. Then you have the commercials in between the news. It's not fake news, its NO NEWS! Then theres reality news shows. Then the exposes or investigative report. Always someone else in the hot seat. News is big business. 24 hours a day 7 days a week. The world never sleeps. Have you ever been to an event or happening that was covered by the news. Was it accurately reported? They want to tell you what happened. The biggest stories in the history of mankind have never been told by the major news media.

Do this little experiment. For 2 full weeks, do not watch, listen or read the news. Then after the two weeks are up turn it all back on. It will still be there. You will realize that you missed absolutely nothing at all. Your life will be less stressful and your blood pressure will be down. Only the Few will be able to do this exercise.

The many cannot. For in this 2 weeks they will be forced to look in at themselves. Who and what they are. They will be forced by there own observation to go back to the news and get their minds off themselves. They need the circus because they are a part of the circus.

> **"Turn off all your news devices for 2 weeks. Then turn them all back on. You will find you missed nothing"**
> **- Phillip Gargoline**

Again, Always be grateful

Be grateful for what you have. Never compare yourself to others.

There will always be people who seem to have more than you or less than you. Whatever your station be grateful to what you have. Always strive for improvement. But at all times be grateful.

We take so much for granted. When you become grateful, your life will become a lot better. Less stressful and far happier. <u>You will even sleep better</u>.

> **"Gratitude is not only the greatest of all virtues, but the parent of all others."**
> **- Cicero**

Never be prejudice

No one picks the color they are or the sex they are. (If we could pick our color, most of us would choose blue.)

> **To quote Dr. Martin Luther King...**
> **"Judge others by the content of their character. Not the color of their skin."**

He is absolutely correct. Judge others by who they are, not what they look like.

In many societies women are treated as un-equals and second class citizens. In dress and in rights. What keeps the western world ahead is that we use **All** of our knowledge and talent. Of both men, women and others. We have 100% of our brainpower contributing to our society.

Some only 50%. Men, women and other's are EQUAL! Judge them for who they are. Prejudice in this world needs to stop before we can advance. If we cannot even accept each other on earth how can we be expected to accept others from the universe.

Patience

You need to be patient in life. Have your plans, your dreams, goals and desires. All of them but be patient. All things in their time.

Things take time to develop into reality. You will find when you achieve parts of your goals that the seeds that made them possible were planted many years ago.

Some by accident or misfortune.

You will realize had that not happened back then, this blessing would not have occurred today.

Be patient, all things in their time. Wait your turn. Respect others. Be patient. Your intuition will tell you when to act. At that time act decisively!

> **"It does not matter how slowly you go, as long as you do not stop." - Confucius**

Do not make things more difficult

Life is difficult enough. Strive to be undifficult. Sometimes this is easy, sometimes this is hard.

Do not be argumentative. State your case and move on. Always try to get to your destination in a straight line. Avoid what will make your journey more difficult. This could be people, work, terrain, doubt. Whatever it is, avoid it and by pass it.

A simple life is the best life. The less you truly need or want the happier you will be. Do not fear being out of vogue or style in where you choose to live, what you wear, what you drive or your work.

As long as you are good with it and you are not hurting others it is good.

By eliminating undue difficulty you will reduce stress and be far happier. A simple example is your drive to and from work. Leave for your job a little earlier or later and leave work a little earlier or later. Whatever works. Try it.

Do not argue with people. Hear what they have to say, really listen, then state what you have to say in a courteous manner. I'm not saying give in. I am saying do not put more fuel on the fire. A fire will not burn without fuel. Sometimes you are better off just holding your tongue and quitely do what you think is best. Make your life less difficult.

> **"Sometimes it is best to ask for forgiveness than permission."**
> **- Admiral Grace Hopper**

Death and old age

A subject only the Few think about. Death comes to us all.

Enjoy your life and do not worry. <u>None of us gets out alive</u>. Death is natural. It is a part of living. Your physical body dies. Your soul, your spirit lives on.

Every religions text will tell you this. The body is only a temporary container. Do not fear death, it will come and you will be fine. It does not matter what religion you are or what you believe. Expect it. It will happen and you will be fine. Unless you have lived a evil life. Getting to death thru old age can be very challenging. For yourself and others. We live a lot longer today. Few realize that in the 1900 the average lifespan for an American was 49 years old. Today due to sanitation, medical advances, inoculation it is much higher. Your youth will determine your old age. Always think long term.

Exercise, stay active, be happy. Do not worry, stress, or hate these are huge killers. Be grateful for what you have and learn to live with less. Not poverty just less stuff. For instance their are people who throw clothes out with the price tags still on them. In your youth, you determine your old age.

> **Again as Cicero wrote in 83 BC**
> **"A life of peace, purity & refinement leads to a calm and untroubled old age"**

As true today as in 83 BC. Let no one tell you different. You determine your old age.

Your life is up to you! My godmother once told me... "It's your life, live it the way you want to." And finally remember, Live a good life, for you will be back again.

> **"Don't forget to live. It's important. -**
> **Laszlo Torzsok**

Just do it!

Be assertive in your life. Follow your own intuition and listen to that inner voice of intuition (some call it conscience). Especially in times of crisis, emergency and life and death situations. You do not have time to think. Just do it! You will know what to do.

Follow your intuition and move quickly. As goes the old saying... "Haste makes waste".

The power is in you to make the correct decisions as if you where on "Auto Pilot". Auto pilot with the universe.

You have to believe!

"You miss 100% of the shots you don't take" Wayne Gretzky, Hockey Great

Change

As stated earlier in this manuscript,

> **"You must grow thru life, not just go thru life!"** - Eric Butterworth

The many aimlessly go thru life. The **FEW** grow thru life.

> **To quote Muhammad Ali....**
> **"A man who views the world at age 50 as they did at age 20 has missed 30 years of his life." - Muhammad Ali**

Change and growth are essential to your happiness, realization and wisdom.

The many never change. that's why they remain in the many. The Few grow, change, acquire wisdom and become intuned with Infinite Intelligence. The universe around us all. Change is essential.

> **"To live is to change and to change often is to become more perfect."**
> **- Cardinal Newman**

Grace

Grace is real. Grace is given to us everyday. The many do not even know grace exists. The Few do, we see it everyday.

M. Scott Peck MD described grace in his best selling book, The Road Less Traveled. I encourage you to read or at least scan this book. In addition to Grace, Dr. Peck also wrote on evolution.... Dr. Peck... "our growth as human beings is being assisted by a force other than our conscious will. To further understand the nature of this force I believe we can benefit from considering yet another miracle, the growth process of all life itself, to which we have given the name evolution" M. Scott Peck MD, The Road Less Traveled page 263.

Grace will come to you, and it will help you if you allow it to. The song "Amazing Grace" will attest to it.

Grace can come to you as something so small as looking for a pen, then spotting one on the ground. Or something as large as spontaneous healing. Grace is, has been and always will be around us all. It is there to help you. To assist you when you need it. Knowing it is there, will help you to recognize and appreciate it. Let me give you one tiny example of how I use grace. Whenever I'm in my car, looking for a parking place I say to myself... "All I need is one". The overwhelming time, like the seas parting a parking space will open up. Try it.

Grace is real, Good is real. And unfortunately Evil is real. Avoid evil at all costs. Nothing good ever comes from evil. It is real and it is the anti-force to grace. If you use grace, then do evil, you will pay a heavy heavy price. Always live your life in the light. Avoid the darkside. Grace is there to help you.

The Four Keys Of The Few

The following 4 sections if acted upon will change and enrich your life.... For the rest of your life!

Meditation

Touched on this earlier in this manuscript. Prayer is when you talk to God, meditation is when you listen to God. To communicate all you need to do is be sincere, be honest, and believe. Remember what the bible says... "only the believers will enter the kingdom of heaven". Only believers can communicate and receive knowledge. Meditation is very simple! It's not chanting, holding your breath, lighting incense, getting in a certain position. It is being quiet, very quiet and still in a quiet place where you will not be interrupted.

This will be very difficult at first. You have never been educated or told to clear your mind. Your mind will run wild the first few times you attempt meditation. Let it run wild. You are unleashing a greater force than you ever knew you had. Why has no one ever taught you this? Because its much like financial education. It's not in the best interest of the many for you to become a self thinker, or financially independent. You have been trained and educated to work and spend for the many. Not yourself. Independent thinkers are dangerous. They cannot be deceived or misled.

Meditation is the first step to becoming one of the Few. Just do it!

"Begin with the end in mind"
- Steven R. Covey

Intuition

I have written earlier on intuition (your third ear). It is so important and vital to your well being I mention it again. This along with meditation is how you get in contact with the universe.

Learn to trust your intuition, your "hunches", your gut instinct. Listen to that little voice within you.

Some call it your conscience and even your guardian angel. It is there for you and you alone.

It is your inner self communicating with you. By just knowing it is there will put you far ahead of the many. (They don't want to communicate with themselves.)

Honing your intuition, improving it is like running or lifting weights. The more time you give it the more you will improve it. Just take the time! Just do it! You will not have to worry about what others say and think because your not going to tell them. If you do, they will only scorn you and hold you back. Remember misery loves company.

Sit quietly and alone and let your intuition work for you. Soon even in this hectic world it will come to you and help you. It is a part of life!

And you are a part of the universe. It's not magic. It's just a fact. Believe in your intuition, follow it, and your life will change for the better. The answers to life are not in the computer, not in your cell phone, not in religion or politics. <u>The answers are within you</u>! Remember we were all made in Gods image. It then follows that we are also made to think and create for a better world in Gods image. More on this to come. Step 1 - Trust your intuition. To quote Napoleon Hill, "What you conceive and believe you can achieve!" It's a universal fact. Genius which we all possess starts with intuition! It is the natural thing to do!

"Genius is only a superior power of seeing" - John Ruskin

"Every living being is an engine geared to the wheelwork of the great universe around us." - Nikola Tesla

---

Infinite Intelligence

We are all part of a great universe. It is one universe. And you are a part of it. The Few know this fact. The many never learn it. Much less ever believe in it. This is what holds them down. Themselves! In his ground breaking book "Think and Grow Rich" Napoleon Hill lays out this secret. He learned it from the great Andrew Carnegie, The self made steel magnate and the richest man (moneywise) of his time. Carnegie wanted to spread his secret to the many in his book "Think and Grow Rich".

The problem is the many never read. So this valuable knowledge sits in every public library in the United States. Unread and still unknown. Until now. You are about to read the greatest secret. It is called **Infinite Intelligence.** The knowledge of man and the entire universe is there for you. For everyone!

Every great thinker or inventor has used this force both knowingly and unknowingly.

Consider this quote by a man who has been called by many the greatest mind of our times.

> **Albert Einstein...** "The intellect has little to do on the road to discovery. There comes a leap on consciousness, call it intuition or what you will and the solution comes to you, and you do not know why or how."

The consciousness and intuition Einstein speaks of is **Infinite Intelligence**. It is known by the Few and unknown to the many. It is when you become a part of the universal intelligence band that surrounds you. Much like radio waves. You cannot see them, yet they are there. Your mind can and will pick up this band if you tune into it. Much like a radio must be tuned in.

This is when you start thinking like a genius. You become a conduit to **Infinite Intelligence**. Your mind becomes one with the universe. This is not difficult. It is really quite natural. Yet only the Few do it. Why? Because you are taught not to use it. Day dreaming, wasted time it is called. Hocus Pocus.

Yet it does work. Consider this quote by the great inventor Nikola Tesla...

> **"Most persons are so absorbed in the contemplation of the outside world, that they are totally oblivious to what is passing on within themselves." - Nikola Tesla**

What Tesla is saying is that you are the greatest power! God is within all of us!

We are all part of God! And this Infinite Intelligence.

There is no greater computer or machine than the spirit and human mind. **The brain is actually a receiver and transmitter.**

This is your contact to Infinite Intelligence. I use the words Infinite Intelligence to define this gift. It also goes by many other names, a few are the holy spirit, the force, intuitions, hunches, a feeling and so on. It's not a question of its presence. The question is why do the many not use it? There is a simple answer to this... Life.

The many lead such hectic lives they do not take time to think. They will tell you they do not have the time, Yet they have time for everything else.

They just live their lives to how they have been taught to live them... Meaningless.

I truly feel for these people. However I cannot reach them.

Hopefully thru this manuscript I can reach you. That is why I am writing it. For You!

Here is another quote by Nikola Tesla that ties everything together "Be alone, that is the secret of invention be alone, that is where ideas are born"

Be alone, quiet, with no distractions ponder and think of what you want or need. The answer will come to you. Maybe not the first, second or third time. But it will come to you. I guarantee it.

What you think is what you become!

As past US President Rutherford B. Hayes said...

"Your Boldest endeavors will be your most successful."

The power is within you! It is within all of us! It is your life, do what you want to do with it. **Always speak and act well**.

And remember the truism...

At any given time, you can go from the many to the Few!

Always, always, always act in the light and use the power of God within you to help yourself and others.

Infinite Intelligence will show you the way. Just believe. Only the believers will be successful.

Again another quote from the one of the greatest inventors and minds of our time...

Nikola Tesla - "My brain is only a receiver. In the universe there is a core from which we obtain knowledge, strength and inspiration."

And this example. Everyone knows that a pencil can write. but can a brand new pencil write? No!

It first must be sharpened. The more you use Infinite Intelligence the sharper and better your mind will become. You will see things far more clearly and find the answers you seek. It is there for you to use!

"I am only a conduit" - John Lennon, Beatles

"The solutions to the problems we face today cannot be solved on the same level of thinking we were at when we created them" - Albert Einstein

"The day science begins to study non physical phenomena it will make more progress in one decade than in all of the previous centuries of its existence." - Nikola Tesla, Inventor

God Yes Yes Yes

God exists! And **YOU** are a part of God!

It is a universal God for every living being in the universe!

This God has been given many names by man. God, Allah, Jehovah, Heavenly Father, Lord, the Supreme being and so on. Yet there is only one God. And this is the God to all of us! God did not create organized religion, man did.

You need no one but yourself to reach God. All you need is to do the right thing, follow your conscience and your Holy Spirit. Practice random acts of kindness. Meditate and pray and thank God every night before you fall asleep and every morning when you awaken. You can even do this while laying down. Your position does not matter. What does matter is your sincerity, belief and what is in your heart.

Simply tell God... Thank you.

That's all it takes.

You will be surprised at what a difference this will make in your life.

Not the end, but the beginning...

By becoming one of the Few you will change our planet and it is our planet.., Earth as we call it, one of billions in the cosmos. **We are not alone, we have never been alone or will be alone.** We are a young species with promise.

The Bible says "The meek shall inherit the earth" the meek are the Few. Non violent, caring, self thinking and one with the universe.

As the 1933 Noble prize winning Physicist Erin Schrodinger stated...

"The total number of minds in the Universe is one"
- Erin Schrodinger, Physicist

We are all a part of that universal mind. And we can all tap into it and become a part of it, thru intuition, Infinite Intelligence, prayer and meditation.

It is not hard, it is simple because it is a part of all of us. **It's natural**. It is the right thing to do! It is what you are meant to become. **It is your destiny.**

Happiness and fulfillment await you. It is your decision. The way is the way of the Few.

> **"When the student is ready, the teacher shall appear" - Buddha**

You hold the teacher in your hands.
I wish you well on this journey we call life.

Michael Gammella

Addendum
I emailed this to my colleagues on the day of my retirement.

Final thoughts at retirement. Be yourself! Know yourself. Know what you want to do and do it. Do not worry about what other people say and do, it is your life, live it your way. Follow your own destiny. Never be jealous, never be envious. Pay yourself first! Save, put money into a blue chip stock index fund. You cannot afford not to. Leave it alone! Let it grow, fund it weekly or monthly. Forget the ups and downs of the market, let your investment ride through good and bad. You will be grateful later. Be thankful you live in America. Half of the world survives on $2.00 a day. Many have never made a phone call. Always strive to do good. Practice random acts of kindness. *1."You want to grow through life, not just go thru life."* Strive to be the most enlightened person you can. Understand your time here is limited. Make the most of it. It is truly up to you. Remember the days drag and the years fly by. Happiness is not a destination

1. Quote from Eric Butterworth

it is a way to live your life. *2. "Someday is not a day of the week."* Be grateful for everything you have. Many people who live in this world cannot turn on a faucet and get water. Do not take things or loved ones for granted. Do not be consumer and luxury driven. You will be surprised how well you can live with less stuff. This will lead to less stress and problems. Simplify your life. Technology is wonderful but don't let it rule you. It is there for you,you are not there for it. Stay healthy, exercise, meditate, have a clear conscience. Do not worry. We spend our lives worrying about things that never happen. Do not let negative energy destroy you. Always focus on the positive the good. Pure love is the greatest strength in the universe. Yes there is an afterlife. Your spirit (soul) lives on. This is why some thing's come naturally to you. You have done them before. Remember at any given time you can go from what you are to what you want to be. It is truly up to you. Follow your passion and dreams. Successful people do. And finally the most important thing. There is an Infinite Intelligence out there. We

2. Quote from Janet Dailey

can all tap into it. We just never take the time or realize it is there. It is there and it has been the secret to my life success and happiness.

I call it the voice. Some call it God, Allah, the force whatever you choose to call it, it is there. Take the time in quiet solitary to access it. Just sit quietly alone and think. You will be amazed how simple it is. Listen to the voice. It will always help you and guide you. Yet few ever take the time to do it. Ignore it at your own peril. Remember prayer is when you talk to God, quiet time (meditation) is when you listen. And remember thought without action is useless. Act on your ideas and dreams. *3. "Your boldest endeavours will be your most successful."* I wish you well on this journey we call life. - Mike Gammella

3. Quote from Rutherford B. Hayes

Made in the USA
Las Vegas, NV
17 October 2023